Healthy Habits

Eat and drink

Sue Barraclough

W
FRANKLIN WATTS
LONDON • SYDNEY

First published in 2010 by
Franklin Watts
338 Euston Road
London NW1 3BH

Franklin Watts Australia
Level 17/207 Kent Street
Sydney NSW 2000

Series editor: Julia Bird
Design: Jane Hawkins
Art director: Jonathan Hair

A CIP catalogue record for this
book is available from the
British Library.

ISBN 978 0 7496 9298 8

Dewey classification: 591'53

Picture credits: Amana Images/Corbis: 9; Daryl Balfour/NHPA: 2,18;
Heide Benser/Corbis: 7; N.A. Callow/NHPA : 21; Jordi Bas Casas/NHPA: 8;
Corbis/Alamy: 13; Laura Eisenburg /istockphoto: 16; Michael & Patricia Fogden/FLPA: 17;
Melvin Grey/NHPA: 10; Franck Guiziou/Hemis/Corbis: 6; JJ Pix/Shutterstock: 22;
Jupiter Images/Creatas/Alamy : front cover tl; Michael Krinke/istockphoto: 19;
Bernard Lacz/NHPA: front cover br; Maximillian Stock/SPL: 23; Monkey Business/
Shutterstock: 1, 4, 11; Tui de Roy/FLPA: 5; Jonathan & Angela Scott/NHPA: 12.
Daniel Sicolo/Design PIcs/Alamy: 20; Richard du Toit/Minden FLPA: 14; Watts PL: 15.

Every attempt has been made to clear copyright. Should there be any inadvertent omission,
please apply to the publisher for rectification.

Printed in China

Franklin Watts is a division of
Hachette Children's Books,
an Hachette UK company.
www.hachette.co.uk

Contents

Eating and drinking   4

Food and energy   6

Feeding and growing   8

Finding food   10

Eating meat   12

Chewing food   14

Swallowing food   16

Drinking water   18

Food and water   20

Tips for healthy eating and drinking   22

Glossary and index   24

Eating and drinking

Humans and other animals need to eat and drink to stay **healthy**. Food and drink keep your body working well. Your body needs a healthy **diet** to grow and repair itself.

Foods such as carrots are good for healthy hair and skin.

4

Wild animals need to live in places where they can find plenty of food and water.

This monkey has climbed a tree to eat some fruit.

Food and energy

All animals need **energy** to make their bodies work and to be **active**. Eating food gives us energy.

A horse needs to eat a lot of grass to keep its body working.

You need to eat a mixture of foods to keep your body fit and healthy.

Cereal is a good food for energy.

Think about it

How do you feel when you are hungry?

Feeding and growing

A baby animal's body is growing fast so it needs lots of food to help it to grow strong and healthy. All female **mammals** make milk to feed their babies.

A dormouse can feed many babies at the same time.

Human babies **suckle** milk from their mothers. Milk is full of **nutrients** that are good for strong bones and teeth.

Babies can also drink milk from a bottle.

 What foods can we make from cow's milk?

Butter, cheese and yoghurt.

9

Finding food

Baby birds need their parents to find them food to eat.

Many animals spend most of the day looking for food. Birds fly around looking for seeds, nuts, worms or small insects to eat and to feed to their young.

Think about it

What are your favourite foods? Why do you like them?

You go to the shops or to markets to buy the food you need. You can help to choose foods that you like.

Fruit gives your body important nutrients.

11

Eating meat

Many animals eat mainly meat. Big cats eat a big meal of meat every few days. Then they rest and sleep until they need to eat again.

Q What is a meat-eating animal called?

A A carnivore.

Lions have sharp, strong teeth for eating meat.

Eating meat gives you useful nutrients, but you only need a little meat in your diet to stay healthy. You also need a mixture of other foods such as fish, cheese, eggs and brown bread, as well as plenty of fruit and vegetables.

A healthy school lunch gives your body the nutrients it needs.

Think about it

How do you feel when you have eaten a big meal?

13

Chewing food

Animals use their teeth to bite and chew their food. Animals that eat mainly meat have sharp, strong teeth to help them bite their food. Animals that eat mainly plants have teeth that are made for grinding and chewing.

 Q What is a plant-eating animal called?

A A herbivore.

A zebra's teeth are shaped to chew tough leaves and grass.

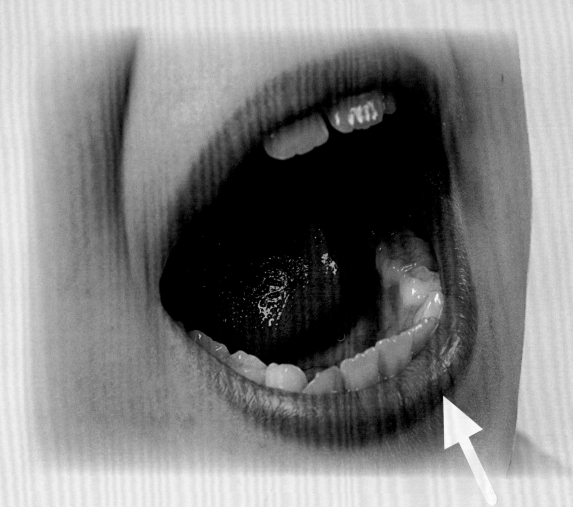

Humans eat both meat and vegetables, so we have a mixture of biting and chewing teeth. The front teeth are mainly used for biting food, the back teeth are mainly used for chewing it.

Humans have a mixture of biting and chewing teeth.

15

Swallowing food

You need to chew and swallow your food so that your body can **digest** it and use it to move, grow and keep warm.

Chewing makes your food easier to swallow.

Snakes can digest all of an animal apart from fur and feathers.

Think about it

What might happen if you swallowed something whole?

Many animals do not have teeth for chewing. A snake has no teeth. It swallows its food whole. The food is slowly broken down inside its body.

Drinking water

All animals need to drink water to stay healthy. Wild animals drink from rivers, lakes and puddles. Some animals have to travel long distances to find water to drink.

Elephants travel many kilometres to find water holes.

You need to drink water every day to keep your body working properly. You need to drink more water when you are active, as you lose water through **sweating**.

Think about it

How do you feel when you are thirsty?

Feeling thirsty is your body's way of telling you to drink some water.

19

Food and water

Most foods have water in them so you can also get water from the foods you eat. Foods such as tomatoes and melons contain lots of water so they are juicy.

You can get water from watermelon, but you still need to drink plenty of water, too.

A bee has a long tongue that helps it to drink nectar.

Some animals feed on nectar. Nectar is a sweet **liquid** found in flowers. Honey bees use nectar to make honey.

Q Which other animals feed on nectar?

A Lots! Butterflies, moths, bats and humming birds for example.

21

Tips for healthy eating and drinking

✓ Drink about 6-8 cups of water every day. You need to drink more during exercise or active play.

✓ Eat at least five portions of different fruit and vegetables every day. A portion is about a handful.

✓ Keep your body at a healthy weight by not eating too much and by playing active games for at least one hour each day.

✓ Remember that no one food can give you all the nutrients you need, so eat a mixture of different foods.

Food and water give you energy to move.

To be healthy, your diet should be mainly **starchy** foods such as potatoes and pasta, along with plenty of fruit and vegetables. You should eat smaller amounts of **dairy foods**, meat, fish, eggs and beans. And even smaller amounts of fatty or salty foods and sweet foods and drinks.

This food plate shows which types of food we should eat most and least of.

Glossary

active able to move or take part in an activity.
dairy foods foods that are made from milk, such as cheese.
diet the types of food a person usually eats.
digest to break down food inside your body.
energy something that makes things work, move or change.
healthy fit and well. A healthy diet is good for you.
liquid a substance that can be poured easily.
mammal an animal that suckles its young.
nutrient a substance that your body needs to live.
starchy filling foods such as bread and potatoes.
suckle to suck or drink milk from the mother.
sweat to lose liquid through your skin.

Index

diet 4
digesting 16, 17

energy 6-7

fruit and vegetables 5, 11, 13, 15, 22, 23

meat 12-13, 23
milk 8, 9, 22

nutrients 9, 11, 13, 22

suckling 8-9
swallowing 16-17

teeth 14-15

water 5, 18-19, 20, 22